Galloping GERTIE

THE TRUE STORY OF THE
TACOMA NARROWS BRIDGE COLLAPSE

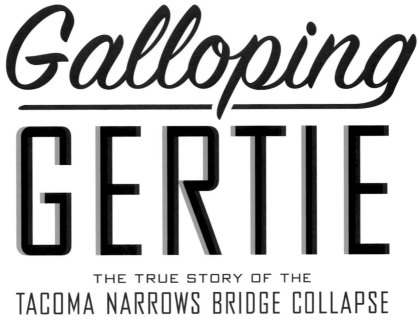

Amanda Abler

Illustrated by
Levi Hastings

little bigfoot
an imprint of sasquatch books
seattle, wa

A New Bridge Opens: Tacoma, Washington, August 1940

Dale Wirsing stepped onto the Tacoma Narrows Bridge for the first time in his life.

Three years in the making, the bridge had just opened the month before, connecting the Kitsap Peninsula to the city of Tacoma, Washington.

Under Dale's feet the roadway of the suspension bridge gently rose and fell, like a boat rolling on the ocean. Far below churned the fierce waters of the Narrows.

Through his living room window, Dale had watched with curiosity as workmen built the bridge towers, strung the cables, and then finally pieced the roadway together high above the water.

How exciting it was to finally walk on the bridge!

But was it normal for such a mammoth bridge to bob and bounce, even on a calm evening such as this?

A local engineer, Clark Eldridge, had designed the bridge to be lightweight and flexible . . . perhaps a little too flexible.

When the wind blew, the center span bounced up and down. The men who built the bridge nicknamed her "Galloping Gertie." People said they could see the cars ahead of them disappear and reappear as they drove across her. Others claimed it was like riding a roller coaster!

Dale didn't know this would not just be his first but his only time walking across her. Nor did he have any idea of the tragedy that would soon befall Gertie in just a few months' time, on his birthday.

Disaster: Thursday, November 7, 1940

Shortly after midnight, a chilly fall wind began to whistle past Dale's house, nestled next to the dark waters of the Tacoma Narrows.

Dale was tucked in bed safe and warm, dreaming of nothing but turning a year older that day.

As Dale slept, Clark Eldridge, the bridge designer, drove across Gertie on his way to work. Gertie's roadway bobbed slowly up and then down, carrying Eldridge's car with it, just like any ordinary day since the opening of the bridge.

By midmorning, Dale was awake. Outside, towering trees swayed under the strength of the wind that had now picked up to over forty miles per hour. But the wind often blasted past Dale's house and howled through the Narrows. Gertie had already survived several fall storms with winds well over fifty miles per hour.

However, Dale wasn't thinking about the wind. He was thinking about his special birthday dinner that night, and what present his dad might bring home for him after work.

As Dale played inside his cozy house, Gertie suddenly began to twist from side to side in the wind. The edges of her center span swung back and forth, rising high into the air.

Gertie was swinging so wildly that no one could drive or even walk on her.

Frightened, the man running Gertie's tollbooth quickly shut the bridge down.

This was little help to the four people who were already crossing Gertie and were now stranded on her center span.

A man and a woman crawled desperately away from their toppled truck toward Gertie's west tower.

Another man, forced to abandon his car with his dog, Tubby, still inside, crawled toward the east tower.

The fourth person was a college student who had walked across Gertie just to enjoy the bounce of her center span.

Gertie swung him so far out, he could see a boat passing under him.

Gertie groaned.

She buckled.

Sounds of cracking concrete echoed around the struggling travelers.

Chunks of her roadway burst out and slipped across her lanes. Lampposts snapped off and rolled about like matchsticks.

SNAP!

CRAACK

CRAAAAACK

Dale's mother glanced out the window, just as a massive piece of concrete fell from Gertie's underbelly and splashed into the water below.

"Dale!" his mom called to him in surprise.

He ran to her and together they watched in amazement as Gertie flailed about in the wind.

To everyone's relief, the winds calmed a bit and so did Gertie.

Two bridge workmen in a truck backed out onto Gertie and picked up the man and the woman.

At Gertie's opposite end, with torn pants and bloodied knees, the college student and the other man reached the east tower safely.

Unfortunately, Tubby, the dog, was still stuck in the car on the bridge. A photographer who had been called to the scene and a professor who happened to be there studying Gertie's movement that day both separately tried to rescue Tubby. But Gertie's swinging, even in calmer winds, was too much and forced the men to turn back.

BRINNNG!

A neighbor was calling from up the street. She had also been watching Gertie. Would Dale and his mother like to come to her house for a better view?

Yes, they would!

What a spectacular birthday this was turning out to be. Dale was full of excitement and had no idea how scared everyone was on the bridge.

As the wind picked up again, they gathered in front of the giant picture window and watched while Gertie whipped around like a flag flapping on a pole.

Gertie twisted one way, which caused her to twist with more force the other way. At last, the strain from all the movements was too much for even the mighty Gertie. Her beams fatigued, she gave in. Her steel girders snapped like rubber bands.

Her bolts shot into the air. The howling wind mixed with the screeching of metal on metal as her steel cables rubbed back and forth, finally breaking and flying free.

A firework of sparks from snapping wires rained down into the Narrows.

Then with one final, frantic twist, Gertie's concrete roadway ripped like paper and she plummeted into the waves below with a massive one-hundred-foot splash.

RRRIP!

SPLASH!

Clark Eldridge had been called to the scene when Gertie first started to swing about. Now he stood white-faced and watched as his beloved bridge disappeared into the churning water below, his heart sinking along with her.

Those who had crawled to safety, as well
as other gathered bystanders, stood back,
heartbroken and in shock.

Gertie appeared heartbroken as well. Her collapsed center span sagged wearily, and her torn roadway dangled like tattered rags into the water.

Safe in his neighbor's house, Dale couldn't believe he had just watched the collapse of the bridge that he had crossed just a few months earlier.

Gertie had only been open for four months.

Still in shock, Dale headed home with his mother.
However, his mind was already meandering back to
his birthday dinner that night.

What a perfect ending it would be
to such an exciting day.

Only when Dale was much older
would he realize what a somber and
frightening event it had been for the
people on the bridge.

**Tacoma Narrows Bridge Opening Day:
Saturday, October 14, 1950**

Almost a decade after Gertie's collapse, teenage
Dale marched steadily across the newly rebuilt
Tacoma Narrows Bridge with Boy Scout Troop 48.
He and his good friend Robert each carried a flag
that flapped in the relentless winds of the Narrows.

Dale was proud to be part of the opening-day ceremony for this
new bridge, which was quickly nicknamed "Sturdy Gertie" because
of her strong design. Sturdy Gertie was not the galloping type.

Tacoma Narrows Bridge and Beyond: 2007–Present

Sturdy Gertie became so busy that in 2007 a second bridge was built right next to her to make room for all the cars. The Tacoma Narrows Bridge now consists of two twin suspension bridges, one carrying eastbound traffic and the other westbound.

Below the Tacoma Narrows Bridge, Galloping Gertie's broken remains still rest underwater, sheltering a variety of marine life.

Her torn roadway and
concrete rubble make a cozy
home for fish, anemones,
sea stars, and crabs, who all need
a resting place from the strong currents. Many giant Pacific
octopuses also make Gertie's remains their home.

To ensure safety, scale models of bridge designs are now tested in wind tunnels to check for stability in all sorts of weather.

Gertie's collapse has helped engineers, teaching them to build safer bridges.

Never again will they build a bridge as flexible as Gertie.

Many years have now passed since Dale was a boy. Often, he visits a cafe perched just up the street from his childhood home. Gazing out over the bridge and enjoying a cup of steaming seafood stew, he will forever be reminded of Galloping Gertie and his fateful birthday.

College student, Howard Clifford, runs for his life as Galloping Gertie begins to collapse.

Why Did Galloping Gertie Collapse?

Clark Eldridge's original design for Galloping Gertie included a twenty-five-foot stiffening **truss** that ran along the underside of the bridge. However, world-famous bridge designer Leon Moisseiff suggested replacing the truss with an eight-foot **plate girder** on the side of the roadway to give the bridge a sleeker look, as well as lower construction costs. Gertie was already extremely flexible because she was the narrowest suspension bridge ever built compared to her length. Removing the truss from the design made her even more flexible and vulnerable to the wind. On the day of Gertie's collapse, a band holding the north cables slipped loose, perhaps from all the movement on previous days. This allowed Gertie to move and twist even more easily.

Engineers and scientists still debate about what caused Gertie to finally collapse. For many years, people believed that **resonance** was to blame. Resonance occurs when a force pushes or pulls on an object, on and off, causing it to vibrate at its **natural frequency**, or the frequency at which it most easily vibrates. For example, a girl pumping her legs on a swing creates a push or a pull at the exact right moment to match the frequency of the swing and therefore makes herself swing higher and higher.

What would resonance have looked like on Gertie? Gusts of wind would have pushed on Gertie at just the right moment, causing her to swing a little farther each time. However, there is one big problem with this idea.

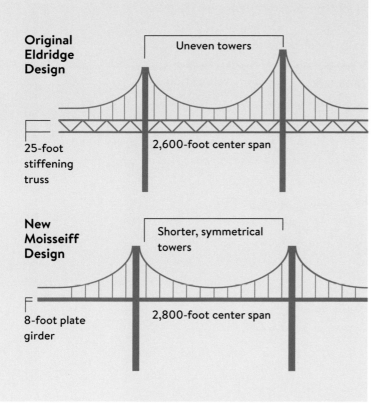

Original
Eldridge
Design

Uneven towers

25-foot
stiffening
truss

2,600-foot center span

New
Moisseiff
Design

Shorter, symmetrical
towers

8-foot plate
girder

2,800-foot center span

Comparison of Clark Eldridge's original bridge design to Leon Moisseiff's modified bridge design

The wind that day blew at a steady forty miles per hour. Without gusts, there was no way for the wind to start and stop pushing on Gertie's roadway to match the natural frequency of her swinging. Therefore, resonance cannot be blamed for Gertie's collapse.

However, because the wind was constant that day, the most likely reason for the collapse was **aeroelastic flutter**—a mathematically complicated concept. To put it simply, all the swinging and twisting in different directions created a rhythm that made Gertie's movements even stronger. Eventually, all the rhythmic motion overcame the strength of her structure and she collapsed.

Trying to Save Gertie

After Gertie opened in 1940, her bouncing and swaying made many Tacomans question her safety. Although the Washington State Department of Transportation assured the public that Gertie was safe to cross, the city's engineers worried. They asked Moisseiff, who had modified Eldridge's original design, what he thought of Gertie's unusual movements. He assured them that Gertie was safe and sturdy.

However, many local engineers remained unconvinced. The Washington State Department of Transportation hired F. B. Farquharson, a professor at the University of Washington, to study Gertie and make a model of her. The professor ran tests on the miniature Gertie in a wind tunnel. He saw the same bouncing on his model that he had seen on the real Gertie. He also saw a new and frightening twisting motion.

The professor instructed the bridge engineers to tie Gertie down with cables to control her movements. However, Gertie continued to bounce even with the cables in place. Next, the professor recommended installing wind deflectors to break up the wind as it blew across Gertie. Sadly, Gertie collapsed before the deflectors could ever be built.

"We knew from the night of the day the bridge opened that something was wrong. On that night the bridge began to gallop."

—**F. B. FARQUHARSON**, *University of Washington professor*

Another Bouncing Bridge?

In June 2000, the Millennium Bridge, a slender metal footbridge, opened in London, England. Although the engineers had carefully designed the bridge, it had to be closed after just two days because of extreme bouncing.

The engineers expected the bridge to bounce a little due to its long, thin structure, however, what they didn't consider was how people would react to this movement. As the bridge swayed slightly, the people on the bridge began to waddle back and forth to steady themselves, walking like penguins. All the people moving together in the same way matched the natural frequency of the bridge, causing the bridge to sway even more through resonance. Eventually, the bridge was closed down until **dampers** could be added to the joints of the bridge to soften the swaying. The bridge reopened in February 2002 and still stands today.

Although the engineers didn't expect people to be waddling in unison, the effect of this type of crowd movement on a bridge has

London Millennium Bridge

been known for hundreds of years. For good reason, it is military tradition that soldiers break step or stop marching in unison before they cross a bridge. On multiple occasions, the vibrations from marching soldiers have caused bridges to collapse through resonance. The soldiers' rhythmic movements caused the bridges to vibrate at their natural frequencies, eventually tearing them apart.

What Happened to Clark Eldridge?

After Gertie's collapse, her designer, Clark Eldridge, decided he needed a break from bridges. He joined the US Navy and moved to Guam in 1941. The United States entered World War II shortly after, and Eldridge was captured by the Japanese. He remained a prisoner for almost four years until the end of the war. During his time in the prison camp, one of the Japanese officers who had studied in the United States recognized him. The officer walked up to Eldridge and said, "Tacoma Bridge!"

Eldridge eventually returned to Tacoma, where he worked as a general contractor and engineer. Even after retiring at age seventy-four, he kept busy, continuing as a consulting engineer for many years.

"I go over the [new] Tacoma Bridge frequently and always with an ache in my heart. It was my bridge."

—**CLARK ELDRIDGE**, *Galloping Gertie's designer*

Does a Giant Octopus Live Below the Tacoma Narrows Bridge?

If you talk to someone from Tacoma, they might tell you the legend of the giant Pacific octopus named King Octopus who lives under the Tacoma Narrows Bridge. People claim to have seen large tentacle-like arms reaching out of the water near the bridge. Divers in these waters have seen plenty of giant Pacific octopuses stretching up to fifteen feet across. If you ever drive over the Tacoma Narrows Bridge, keep an eye out for King!

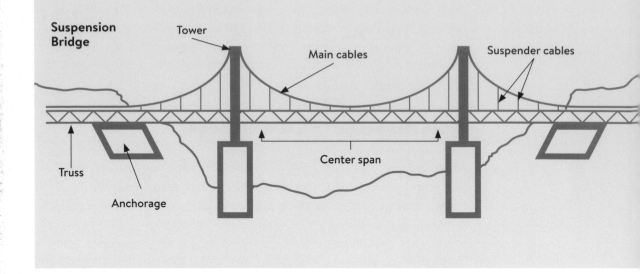

Structure of a Suspension Bridge

On a suspension bridge like Galloping Gertie, the roadway is supported by the main cables that are strung onto two or more towers. At either end of the bridge, the cables are attached to anchorages, or massive blocks of concrete or rock, to secure the cables in place, just as the ropes of a camping tent are staked into the ground. Although the cables might appear to be solid steel, each cable is actually made of thousands of wires all bundled together. Each individual wire on Galloping Gertie was about the thickness of a pencil. It took 14,191 miles of wire to build the 1940 Tacoma Narrows Bridge, enough wire to circle more than halfway around the earth. A suspension bridge is further supported by suspender cables that hang from the main cables down to the roadway. The underside of the roadway is often strengthened by a truss to make the bridge stiffer. This can be especially important under the center span, the section of the bridge between the two towers.

Fun Bridge Videos and Movies to Watch

Search these key words on YouTube to see these bridges in action.

- *Tacoma Narrows Bridge Collapse 1940*: Watch the real Galloping Gertie collapse.

- *London Millennium Bridge Opening*: Watch the bridge sway from the crowd's movement and learn more science about bridges.

- *Millennium Bridge Harry Potter*: Watch the Millennium Bridge imitate Galloping Gertie's twisting in a scene from *Harry Potter and the Half-Blood Prince*. WARNING: This one is a little scary; after all, it is Harry Potter!

Check out this website for a movie about Galloping Gertie.

- Visit CarlyVester.com to watch the trailer for *700 Feet Down*, a documentary about the history and the wreckage of Galloping Gertie, and to find information about how to watch the full movie.

Glossary

AEROELASTIC FLUTTER: extreme and increasing instability caused by the pairing of two or more of an object's vibrations in different directions with similar natural frequencies due to the constant flow of liquid or gas around the object

DAMPER: a device used to reduce mechanical vibration

NATURAL FREQUENCY: the frequency at which an object most easily vibrates

PLATE GIRDER: a steel beam built from plates welded or riveted together

RESONANCE (IN A MECHANICAL SYSTEM): an event in which an object vibrates at its natural frequency due to a force pushing or pulling on that object at that same frequency

TRUSS: a sturdy framework used to support, strengthen, or stiffen a bridge or other structure

To my family for the many bridges they create in my life —AA

For my husband, Demetrios, who is always my strongest support,
especially when the storms roll in —LH

Manufactured in China by C&C Offset Printing Co. Ltd.
Shenzhen, Guangdong Province, in April 2021

LITTLE BIGFOOT with colophon is a registered trademark
of Penguin Random House LLC

25 24 23 22 21   9 8 7 6 5 4 3 2 1

Editors: Christy Cox and Ben Clanton
Production editor: Bridget Sweet
Designer: Tony Ong
Photographs: Photo on page 42 courtesy of University of Washington
Libraries, Special Collections, UW 20731; photo on page 44 © Acabashi,
Creative Commons CC-BY-SA 4.0, Wikimedia Commons
https://commons.wikimedia.org/w/index.php?curid=86463207

Library of Congress Cataloging-in-Publication Data
Names: Abler, Amanda, author. | Hastings, Levi, illustrator.
Title: Galloping Gertie : the true story of the Tacoma Narrows Bridge
collapse / Amanda Abler ; illustrated by Levi Hastings.
Description: Seattle, WA : Little Bigfoot, 2021. | Includes bibliographical
references. | Audience: Ages 8-12 | Audience: Grades 4-6
Identifiers: LCCN 2020037253 | ISBN 9781632172631 (hardcover)
Subjects: LCSH: Tacoma Narrows Bridge (Tacoma, Wash. : 1940)--Juvenile
literature. | Bridge failures--Washington (State)--Tacoma
Narrows--Juvenile literature.
Classification: LCC TG24.W3 A63 2021 | DDC 363.12/5--dc23
LC record available at https://lccn.loc.gov/2020037253

ISBN: 978-1-63217-263-1

Sasquatch Books
1904 Third Avenue, Suite 710
Seattle, WA 98101

SasquatchBooks.com